CREE B GOOD

SUPER PHONICS

SUPER PHONICS: 12 INTERACTIVE LESSONS & GAMES TO BOOST READING SKILLS AND HAVE FUN!

First published by Camp Wanderlust 2024

Copyright © 2024 by CREE B GOOD

All rights reserved. No part of this publication may be reproduced, stored or transmitted in any form or by any means, electronic, mechanical, photocopying, recording, scanning, or otherwise without written permission from the publisher. It is illegal to copy this book, post it to a website, or distribute it by any other means without permission.

CREE B GOOD asserts the moral right to be identified as the author of this work.

CREE B GOOD has no responsibility for the persistence or accuracy of URLs for external or third-party Internet Websites referred to in this publication and does not guarantee that any content on such Websites is, or will remain, accurate or appropriate.

Designations used by companies to distinguish their products are often claimed as trademarks. All brand names and product names used in this book and on its cover are trade names, service marks, trademarks and registered trademarks of their respective owners. The publishers and the book are not associated with any product or vendor mentioned in this book. None of the companies referenced within the book have endorsed the book.

First edition

ISBN: 979-8-9919447-1-7

This book was professionally typeset on Reedsy.
Find out more at reedsy.com

*My precious son, Baby Born, inspired me to embrace the journey of education
and face life's challenges head-on. When the NICU doctors had their doubts, it
was your boundless spirit that pushed me to believe in your potential
and guide you to conquer those obstacles and leave
your own unique imprint on the world.
-Super Mommy*

Every word is a puzzle, every sound a clue—
together, let's unlock the magic of reading, me
and you!

CREED B GOOD

Contents

Foreword	ii
Preface	iii
Acknowledgments	v
How to Use	1
Tips: Tips for Parents and Educators	4
Unit 1: Single Consonant Sounds	6
Unit 2: Short Vowel Sounds	9
Unit 3: Short Vowels and CVC Blends	12
Unit 4: Consonant Digraphs and Blends	16
Unit 5: Long Vowel Sounds and Blending	20
Unit 6: Vowel Digraphs and Diphthongs	24
Unit 7: Silent Letter: Magic E	28
Unit 8: Special Consonants	33
Unit 9: R-Controlled Vowels	36
Unit 10: Syllables and Multi-syllabic Words	40
Unit 11: Irregular Words and Sight Words	44
Unit 12: Reading Practice—Sentences	47
Congratulations!	50
Bonus: Long Vowel Study Cards	54
About the Author	206

Foreword

Learning to read is one of life's most empowering skills, and this phonics book was born from my journey as a parent determined to help my own children overcome learning challenges. With two wonderful kids, each with unique needs and learning styles, I found that traditional methods weren't always enough to keep them engaged and progressing. So, I set out to create a learning approach to make reading accessible, exciting, and achievable for them and other children.

This book was crafted to be more than just a teaching tool—it's meant to be a source of encouragement and confidence for children of all backgrounds. With step-by-step guidance, engaging activities, and a fun approach, my hope is that children using this book will not only learn to read but also develop a genuine love for it.

If you're a parent, teacher, or caregiver reading this, I want to thank you for trusting this book on your journey with your child. Together, we can nurture a lifetime of curiosity, confidence, and literacy. I hope this phonics guide inspires joy and success for your child, just as it has for mine.

Happy reading and happy learning!

Preface

As a mother of two extraordinary children, I've experienced firsthand the transformative power of phonics in teaching reading skills. My journey with this approach began over two years ago when I developed this phonics guide with my own children in mind, and I've spent the past two years using and refining it as they learned. The results have been deeply rewarding.

My youngest, now 7 years old, is energetic and would likely be labeled as having ADHD if he were in a traditional school setting. My eldest, now 12, was born with a grade 4 bilateral brain hemorrhage, making classroom learning an uphill battle at times. Both of them have thrived with a phonics-based reading approach, and this book captures the methods I used to help them succeed.

Choosing to homeschool them was a deeply personal decision. I wanted to offer each child a customized approach to learning tailored to their unique needs. My youngest required interactive, engaging lessons that matched his lively personality, while my eldest needed a calm, steady approach to support him in overcoming learning obstacles.

After extensive research into effective teaching methods, I discovered phonics as a structured, logical approach to reading. Phonics helps children understand the relationship between letters and sounds, enabling them to decode words and read fluently. It's a process that breaks reading down into manageable steps, helping them build confidence and skill at their own pace.

For my 7-year-old, phonics has been a way to channel his energy into hands-on activities that make learning fun. Using movement, games, and multisensory techniques, I created lessons that keep him engaged and eager to learn. This approach transformed learning into an adventure.

My 12-year-old's journey with phonics has been nothing short of inspiring. Despite his early medical challenges, he's become a confident, proficient reader. With consistent practice and a customized approach, he mastered reading, pursued advanced courses, and maintained a 4.0 GPA in public school, eventually taking on college-level studies.

This book is the product of two years of real-world application and observation, during which I saw my children surpass their challenges and thrive academically. Phonics has been foundational to their success, providing a strong base for their academic futures. My hope is that this guide will empower other parents and educators to help their children reach their full potential, no matter what obstacles may lie ahead.

Acknowledgments

This book is truly a labor of love, and I couldn't have brought it to life without the incredible support of so many people.

First and foremost, I want to thank my children, whose resilience and enthusiasm inspired every page. Watching them grow and succeed through this approach has been my greatest reward.

I extend a huge thank you to my Camp Wanderlust family and friends for their encouragement and belief in my vision. Your advice, patience, and unwavering enthusiasm kept me motivated through every step of this journey.

To the educators and specialists who generously shared their insights on phonics and child literacy—thank you. Your expertise helped me shape this book into a resource that can serve children of all learning styles and needs.

Lastly, my heartfelt thanks go to the families and educators using this book to support their young readers. I hope it brings you joy, progress, and many memorable learning moments.

How to Use

This phonics workbook has been designed to provide a comprehensive and engaging learning experience for children of various ages and abilities. To ensure that your child benefits from this resource, follow the detailed instructions below on using this workbook effectively.

Assess your child's current level: Before starting the workbook, assess your child's current reading level and familiarity with phonics. This will help you identify the appropriate starting point and tailor the lessons to meet your child's specific needs.

Work at a comfortable pace: Progress through the workbook at a pace that suits your child's learning style and capabilities. You may need to spend more time on certain concepts or revisit previous lessons to reinforce understanding. Remember, it's important to be patient and flexible in your approach.

Use a systematic approach: The workbook is organized into chapters that build upon one another, introducing new concepts while reinforcing previously learned skills. Begin with the first chapter and work your way through the chapters sequentially. This will ensure a solid understanding of each phonics concept.

Encourage active participation: Engage your child in each lesson by encouraging them to read aloud, write, and participate in activities. Active participation helps to reinforce learning and improve retention of the material.

Utilize multi-sensory techniques: Incorporate various multi-sensory techniques such as visual aids, auditory input, and tactile activities to enhance your child's learning experience. This approach caters to different learning styles and helps to maintain interest and engagement.

Review and practice regularly: Regular review and practice are crucial for mastering phonics concepts. Set aside time each day to work on the workbook and encourage your child to practice reading and writing independently. Revisit previous lessons as needed to reinforce understanding.

Monitor progress and provide feedback: Keep track of your child's progress and celebrate their achievements. Provide constructive feedback and support to help them overcome any difficulties they may encounter. Adjust your approach as necessary to ensure your child continues to make progress.

Supplement with additional resources: While this workbook provides a comprehensive phonics curriculum, you may wish to supplement your child's learning with our additional resources, such as flashcards, games, or online tools. These can provide extra practice and further reinforce the concepts learned in the workbook.

Communicate with your child: Maintain an open line of communication with your child throughout the learning process. Discuss their feelings, successes, and challenges. This will help you better understand their needs and tailor the lessons accordingly.

By following these detailed instructions, you can maximize the benefits of this phonics workbook and provide your child with the tools they need to develop strong reading skills. With patience, persistence, and a positive

HOW TO USE

attitude, your child will make significant progress and experience the joy of reading.

Tips: Tips for Parents and Educators

Supporting students in their journey to become proficient readers is a crucial role for parents and educators. Here are some tips to help you effectively guide your child or student through the process of learning phonics:

Set realistic expectations: Understand that every child learns independently and has unique strengths and weaknesses. Be patient and set realistic expectations based on their individual abilities. Celebrate their achievements and progress, no matter how small.

Create a positive learning environment: Establish a comfortable and distraction-free space for learning. Encourage a growth mindset by praising effort and persistence rather than just results. This will help your child feel supported and motivated to keep trying, even when faced with challenges.

Make learning fun and engaging: Incorporate games, songs, and hands-on activities into your phonics lessons to make learning more enjoyable. This not only helps to maintain your child's interest and engagement but also reinforces the concepts they're learning.

Be consistent and persistent: Consistency is key when teaching phonics. Set aside regular time for practice and stick to a routine. Consistent practice helps to build and reinforce your child's phonics skills, ultimately leading to better reading proficiency.

Encourage reading outside of lessons: Foster a love for reading by providing your child with various books, magazines, and other reading materials. Encourage them to read for pleasure and explore different genres to expand their vocabulary and reinforce phonics skills.

Model good reading habits: Demonstrate good reading habits by reading aloud to your child or having them read along with you. This helps to expose them to correct pronunciation, intonation, and expression, which are essential components of fluent reading.

Offer individualized support: Identify and address any specific challenges your child may face in their phonics learning. Provide targeted support and guidance to help them overcome these obstacles and build their confidence.

Monitor progress and adjust as needed: Regularly assess your child's progress and adjust your teaching approach as needed. This ensures that you are meeting their needs and providing the appropriate level of support and challenge.

Collaborate with other educators and professionals: If you're an educator, collaborate with colleagues, special education professionals, or other experts to share ideas, resources, and strategies for supporting students in their phonics learning. This will help you stay informed and provide the best possible instruction for your students.

Maintain open communication: Keep the lines of communication open with your child or student. Encourage them to share their thoughts, feelings, and concerns about their phonics learning. This will help you understand their needs and adjust your teaching approach accordingly.

By following these tips, parents and educators can provide effective support and guidance to help students develop strong phonics skills and become confident, fluent readers.

Unit 1: Single Consonant Sounds

Objective: Students will learn the single consonant sounds of the English language, and practice writing them. Students must master each consonant sound before moving on to the next chapter.

Materials:

- Flashcards of single consonant sounds
- Images or objects representing words with consonant sounds
- Worksheets for practice exercises
- Whiteboard or blackboard and markers or chalk

Introduction (5 minutes):

1. Write the following single consonant sounds on the board: **m, t, s, r, p, n, c, k, b, d, f, h, l, v, w, j, x, y, z, q, g.**
2. Explain to students that these are the consonant sounds they will learn in this unit, and they will be introduced in an order that helps them learn most effectively.
3. **Direct Instruction (15 minutes):**
4. Start with the first consonant sound, 'm'.
5. Show a flashcard with the letter 'm' and pronounce the /m/ sound.
6. Show images or objects representing words with the 'm' sound (e.g., monkey, map, and moon).
7. Ask students to repeat the /m/ sound and identify it in the example words.

8. Write the example words on the board, underlining the 'm' sound in each word.
9. Repeat the process for the remaining consonant sounds.

Guided Practice (15 minutes):

1. Divide students into pairs.
2. Distribute worksheets with practice exercises that include identifying and writing single consonant sounds.
3. Instruct students to work with their partners to complete the exercises.
4. Walk around the room, providing assistance and guidance as needed.

Independent Practice (10 minutes):

1. Ask students to work individually on a new set of worksheets that require them to identify and write single consonant sounds.
2. Encourage students to refer to the consonant sounds and example words on the board if they need help.

Closure (5 minutes):

1. Review the consonant sounds, asking students to say each sound aloud and provide an example word.
2. Collect the worksheets and provide feedback on students' progress.
3. **Assessment:** Evaluate students' understanding of single consonant sounds based on their participation during the lesson and their performance on the worksheets.

Game-time: Scavenger Hunt (Consonants)
Materials:

- Alphabet flashcards

- A small bag or container to hold the flashcards

Instructions:

1. Spread the flashcards face down on a table or the floor.
2. Have the child choose a flashcard from the bag or container and say the letter name and sound.
3. Set a timer for 30 seconds and challenge the child to find an object in the room that starts with the sound of the chosen letter.
4. When the timer goes off, the child should show the object they found and say its name and the sound of the starting letter.
5. Repeat the game with different flashcards.

Variations:

- To make the game more challenging, you can use digraphs, blends, or other phonics concepts instead of individual letters.
- You can play this game with multiple children by having them race to find objects that start with the chosen sound.
- You can also use this game as a spelling activity by having the child spell out the name of the object they found using the flashcards.

Note: Do not move to the next unit until this lesson is mastered.

Unit 2: Short Vowel Sounds

Objective: Students will learn the short vowel sounds (a, e, i, o, u), recognize them in words, and practice writing them. Students must master each short vowel sound before moving on to the next chapter.

Materials:

- Flashcards of short vowel sounds
- Images or objects representing words with the short vowel sounds
- Worksheets for practice exercises
- Whiteboard and markers

Introduction (5 minutes):

1. Write the short vowel sounds on the board: a, e, i, o, u.
2. Explain to students that these are short vowel sounds, and they will be introduced with examples and images to help them understand and remember the sounds.

Direct Instruction (15 minutes):

1. Start with the first short vowel sound, 'a'.
2. Show a flashcard with the letter 'a' and pronounce the /ă/ sound.
3. Show images or objects representing words with the 'a' sound (e.g., cat, hat, and apple).
4. Ask students to repeat the /ă/ sound and identify it in the example

words.
5. Write the example words on the board, underlining the 'a' sound in each word.
6. Repeat the process for the remaining short vowel sounds (e, i, o, u).

Guided Practice (15 minutes):

1. Divide students into pairs.
2. Distribute worksheets with practice exercises that include identifying and writing short vowel sounds.
3. Instruct students to work with their partners to complete the exercises.
4. Walk around the room, providing assistance and guidance as needed.

Independent Practice (10 minutes):

1. Ask students to work individually on a new set of worksheets that require them to identify and write short vowel sounds.
2. Encourage students to refer to the short vowel sounds and example words on the board if they need help.

Closure (5 minutes):

1. Review the short vowel sounds, asking students to say each sound aloud and provide an example word.
2. Collect the worksheets and provide feedback on students' progress.
3. Remind students that they should not move on to the next chapter until they have mastered the current lesson. Continuously assess their understanding and provide additional practice exercises as needed.

Assessment: Evaluate students' understanding of short vowel sounds based on their participation during the lesson and their performance on the worksheets. Make sure students have a strong grasp of the current lesson before proceeding to the next chapter.

UNIT 2: SHORT VOWEL SOUNDS

Game-time: Bingo (Short Vowels)
Materials:

- Bingo cards with pictures of objects that have short vowel sounds (e.g., cat, bed, box, mug, hen)
- Markers (e.g., coins, buttons, or bingo chips)

Instructions:

1. Give each player a bingo card and a marker.
2. Call out a word from the list of short vowel words (cat, bed, box, mug, hen).
3. If a player has a picture of the word on their bingo card, they cover it with a marker.
4. Continue calling out words until a player gets a straight line (horizontally, vertically, or diagonally) of covered squares and calls out "Bingo!"
5. The first player to call out "Bingo!" wins the game.

Variations:

- To make the game more challenging, you can use words with multiple short vowel sounds or words that have consonant blends.
- You can also play this game in teams, with each team sharing a bingo card and taking turns marking the squares.
- Another variation is to have the players say the sound of the short vowel word they covered when marking it on their bingo card. This helps reinforce the concept of phonics while playing the game.

Note: Do not move to the next unit until this lesson is mastered.

Unit 3: Short Vowels and CVC Blends

Objective: Students will understand the concept of blending sounds in CVC words, practice blending, and improve their reading fluency.

Materials:

- Flashcards of short vowel sounds and consonants
- Images or objects representing CVC words
- Worksheets for practice exercises
- Whiteboard or blackboard and markers or chalk
- Audio recordings of CVC words (optional)

Introduction (5 minutes):

1. Review the short vowel sounds and CVC words taught in the previous lesson.
2. Introduce the concept of blending, explaining that it involves smoothly combining the individual sounds in a word to read it correctly.

Direct Instruction (15 minutes):

1. Write a CVC word on the board (e.g., cat).
2. Model how to blend the sounds in the word by slowly saying each sound and then smoothly combining them: /c/ - /a/ - /t/ > cat.
3. Explain that blending helps improve reading fluency and makes it easier to understand words.

4. Repeat the process with several more CVC words, emphasizing the blending of sounds.

Guided Practice (20 minutes):

1. Divide students into pairs or small groups.
2. Distribute flashcards with consonants and short vowel sounds.
3. Instruct students to take turns creating CVC words with their flashcards and practicing blending the sounds together.
4. Encourage students to help each other with blending and provide assistance as needed.
5. Optionally, play audio recordings of CVC words and have students practice blending the sounds they hear.

Independent Practice (10 minutes):

1. Ask students to work individually on a new set of worksheets that require blending the sounds in CVC words.
2. Encourage students to sound out each letter slowly and then blend the sounds together to read the words.
3. Provide support and guidance as needed, ensuring that students understand the blending process.

Closure (5 minutes):

1. Review the importance of blending in reading fluency and comprehension.
2. Ask students to share their favorite CVC words from the lesson and practice blending the sounds together as a class.
3. Remind students to continue practicing blending sounds when reading at home and in future lessons.

Assessment: Evaluate students' understanding of blending and their ability to apply this skill when reading CVC words based on their participation during the lesson and their performance on the worksheets. Ensure students have a strong grasp of blending before proceeding to more complex phonics concepts.

Game-time: Word Match (Short Vowels)
Materials:

- A set of picture cards with short vowel CVC (consonant-vowel-consonant) words (e.g., cat, bed, box, rug, pin, hat)
- A set of letter cards with the consonants and vowels needed to spell the CVC words
- A tray or flat surface to arrange the cards

Instructions:

1. Shuffle the picture cards and letter cards separately and place them in two stacks face down.
2. Have the player pick a picture card from the stack and identify the word on the card.
3. Have the player choose the letter cards needed to spell the word and place them next to the picture card.
4. Repeat the process with different picture cards.
5. The game is over once all the picture cards have been matched with the correct letter cards.

Variations:

- To make the game more challenging, you can use words with blends or digraphs or longer words with multiple CVC patterns.
- You can also play this game in teams, with each team working together to match the picture cards with the correct letter cards.
- Another variation is to have the players say the word out loud and then

UNIT 3: SHORT VOWELS AND CVC BLENDS

break it down into its individual sounds (phonemes) to reinforce phonics concepts.

Note: Do not move to the next unit until this lesson is mastered.

Unit 4: Consonant Digraphs and Blends

Objective: Students will learn to identify and understand consonant digraphs and blends, practice reading and writing them, and improve their overall phonics knowledge.

Materials:

- Flashcards with consonant digraphs (e.g., ch, sh, th, wh, ph) and blends (e.g., bl, cl, fl, gl, pl, br, cr, dr, fr, gr)
- Images or objects representing words with digraphs and blends
- Worksheets for practice exercises
- Whiteboard or blackboard and markers or chalk
- Audio recordings of words with digraphs and blends (optional)

Introduction (5 minutes):

1. Review the short vowel sounds, CVC words, and blending skills taught in previous lessons.
2. Introduce the concept of consonant digraphs and blends, explaining that digraphs are two consonants that together make one sound, while blends are two or more consonants that make distinct but closely connected sounds.

Direct Instruction (15 minutes):

1. Write a list of common consonant digraphs (e.g., ch, sh, th, wh, ph) and

blends (e.g., bl, cl, fl, gl, pl, br, cr, dr, fr, gr) on the board.
2. Model how to pronounce each digraph and blend, using examples and images to illustrate their sounds in words (e.g., chair for "ch," ship for "sh," etc.).
3. Encourage students to repeat the sounds and practice saying example words.

Guided Practice (20 minutes):

1. Divide students into pairs or small groups.
2. Distribute flashcards with consonant digraphs and blends.
3. Instruct students to take turns creating words with their flashcards, practicing reading and pronouncing digraphs and blends correctly.
4. Encourage students to help each other and provide assistance as needed.
5. Optionally, play audio recordings of words with digraphs and blends and have students practice identifying and pronouncing them.

Independent Practice (10 minutes):

1. Ask students to work individually on a new set of worksheets that require them to read, identify, and write words with consonant digraphs and blends.
2. Encourage students to apply their knowledge of digraphs and blends to read words accurately.
3. Provide support and guidance as needed, ensuring that students understand the concepts of digraphs and blends.

Closure (5 minutes):

1. Review the importance of consonant digraphs and blends in reading fluency and comprehension.
2. Ask students to share their favorite words with digraphs and blends from the lesson and practice pronouncing them as a class.

3. Remind students to continue practicing digraphs and blends when reading at home and in future lessons.

Assessment: Evaluate students' understanding of consonant digraphs and blends and their ability to apply this knowledge when reading and writing words based on their participation during the lesson and their performance on the worksheets. Ensure students have a strong grasp of digraphs and blends before proceeding to more complex phonics concepts.

Game-time: Go Fish (Consonant Digraphs)
Materials:

- A set of cards with words that contain consonant digraphs and blends (e.g., chop, frog, swim, brush, snack, grip, sled, play, flag, brick, clap, trip)
- Two or more players
- A tray or flat surface to arrange the cards

Instructions:

1. Shuffle the cards and deal five cards to each player.
2. Place the remaining cards face down in a stack in the middle of the playing area.
3. The first player asks another player if they have a card with a specific digraph or blend that they need to complete a word in their hand (e.g., "Do you have any cards with 'ch'?").
4. If the player has the requested card, they must give it to the first player. If not, they tell the first player to "go fish" and the first player must draw a card from the stack.
5. If the first player completes a word with the cards in their hand, they place the word on the tray or flat surface.
6. The game continues until all the words have been completed or until there are no more cards left in the stack.
7. The player with the most completed words at the end of the game wins.

UNIT 4: CONSONANT DIGRAPHS AND BLENDS

Variations:

- To make the game more challenging, you can use longer words or words with multiple digraphs or blends.
- You can also change the game to match pairs of digraph or blend cards instead of completing words.
- Another variation is to have players spell out the words on their completed words tray to reinforce phonics concepts.

Note: Do not move to the next unit until this lesson is mastered.

Unit 5: Long Vowel Sounds and Blending

Objective: Students will learn to identify and understand long vowel sounds and their various spelling patterns, practice reading and writing long vowel words, and improve their blending skills.

Materials:

- Flashcards with long vowel sounds and spelling patterns (e.g., a_e, ai, ay, e_e, ee, ea, i_e, ie, igh, o_e, oa, ow, u_e, ue, ew)
- Images or objects representing words with long vowel sounds
- Worksheets for practice exercises
- Whiteboard or blackboard and markers or chalk
- Audio recordings of words with long vowel sounds (optional)

Introduction (5 minutes):

1. Review the short vowel sounds, CVC words, consonant digraphs, and blends taught in previous lessons.
2. Introduce the concept of long vowel sounds, explaining that they are vowels that say their own name.

Direct Instruction (15 minutes):

1. Write a list of long vowel sounds and their spelling patterns (e.g., a_e, ai, ay, e_e, ee, ea, i_e, ie, igh, o_e, oa, ow, u_e, ue, ew) on the board.
2. Model how to pronounce each long vowel sound, using examples and

UNIT 5: LONG VOWEL SOUNDS AND BLENDING

images to illustrate their sounds in words (e.g., cake for "a_e," bead for "ea," etc.).
3. Encourage students to repeat the sounds and practice saying example words.

Guided Practice (20 minutes):

1. Divide students into pairs or small groups.
2. Distribute flashcards with long vowel sounds and spelling patterns.
3. Instruct students to take turns creating words with their flashcards, practicing reading and pronouncing long vowel sounds correctly.
4. Encourage students to help each other and provide assistance as needed.
5. Optionally, play audio recordings of words with long vowel sounds and have students practice identifying and pronouncing them.

Independent Practice (10 minutes):

1. Ask students to work individually on a new set of worksheets that require them to read, identify, and write words with long vowel sounds.
2. Encourage students to apply their knowledge of long vowel sounds and spelling patterns to read words accurately.
3. Provide support and guidance as needed, ensuring that students understand the concepts of long vowel sounds and blending.

Closure (5 minutes):

- Review the importance of long vowel sounds and blending in reading fluency and comprehension.
- Ask students to share their favorite words with long vowel sounds from the lesson and practice pronouncing them as a class.
- Remind students to continue practicing long vowel sounds and blending when reading at home and in future lessons.
- Assessment: Evaluate students' understanding of long vowel sounds and

their ability to apply this knowledge when reading and writing words based on their participation during the lesson and their performance on the worksheets. Ensure students have a strong grasp of long vowel sounds and blending before proceeding to more complex phonics concepts.

Game-time: Word Builder (Long Vowel)
Materials:

- A set of cards with words that contain long vowel sounds and blends (e.g., boat, mail, goat, train, sheep, bread, stain, climb)
- A set of letter cards with the consonants and vowels needed to spell the words on the word cards
- A tray or flat surface to arrange the cards

Instructions:

1. Shuffle the word cards and letter cards separately and place them in two stacks face down.
2. Have the player pick a word card from the stack and identify the word on the card.
3. Have the player choose the letter cards needed to spell the word and place them next to the word card to build the word.
4. Repeat the process with different word cards.
5. Once all the word cards have been matched with the correct letter cards, the game is over.

Variations:

- To make the game more challenging, you can use longer words or words with multiple long vowel sounds or blends.
- You can also play this game in teams, with each team working together

to build the words.
- Another variation is to have the players say the word out loud and then break it down into its individual sounds (phonemes) to reinforce phonics concepts.

Note: Do not move to the next unit until this lesson is mastered.

Unit 6: Vowel Digraphs and Diphthongs

Objective: Students will learn to identify and understand vowel digraphs and diphthongs, practice reading and writing words containing these patterns, and improve their blending skills.

Materials:

- Flashcards with vowel digraphs (ai, ea, oa, ee, etc.) and diphthongs (oi, oy, ou, ow, etc.)
- Images or objects representing words with vowel digraphs and diphthongs
- Worksheets for practice exercises
- Whiteboard or blackboard and markers or chalk
- Audio recordings of words with vowel digraphs and diphthongs (optional)

Introduction (5 minutes):

1. Review the concepts of long vowel sounds, blending, and consonant digraphs from previous lessons.
2. Introduce the concept of vowel digraphs and diphthongs, explaining that vowel digraphs are two vowels that create one sound and diphthongs are vowel combinations that produce a unique sound.

Direct Instruction (15 minutes):

UNIT 6: VOWEL DIGRAPHS AND DIPHTHONGS

1. Write a list of vowel digraphs (ai, ea, oa, ee, etc.) and diphthongs (oi, oy, ou, ow, etc.) on the board.
2. Model how to pronounce each vowel digraph and diphthong, using examples and images to illustrate their sounds in words (e.g., rain for "ai," boat for "oa," coin for "oi," etc.).
3. Encourage students to repeat the sounds and practice saying example words.

Guided Practice (20 minutes):

1. Divide students into pairs or small groups.
2. Distribute flashcards with vowel digraphs and diphthongs.
3. Instruct students to take turns creating words with their flashcards, practicing reading and pronouncing vowel digraphs and diphthongs correctly.
4. Encourage students to help each other and provide assistance as needed.
5. Optionally, play audio recordings of words with vowel digraphs and diphthongs and have students practice identifying and pronouncing them.

Independent Practice (10 minutes):

1. Ask students to work individually on a new set of worksheets that require them to read, identify, and write words with vowel digraphs and diphthongs.
2. Encourage students to apply their knowledge of vowel digraphs and diphthongs to read words accurately.
3. Provide support and guidance as needed, ensuring that students understand the concepts of vowel digraphs and diphthongs.

Closure (5 minutes):

1. Review the importance of vowel digraphs and diphthongs in reading

fluency and comprehension.
2. Ask students to share their favorite words with vowel digraphs and diphthongs from the lesson and practice pronouncing them as a class.
3. Remind students to continue practicing vowel digraphs and diphthongs when reading at home and in future lessons.

Assessment: Evaluate students' understanding of vowel digraphs and diphthongs and their ability to apply this knowledge when reading and writing words based on their participation during the lesson and their performance on the worksheets. Ensure students have a strong grasp of vowel digraphs and diphthongs before proceeding to more complex phonics concepts.

Game-time: Hangman (Vowel Digraphs and Diphthongs)
Materials:

- A list of words that contain vowel digraphs and diphthongs (e.g., boat, coin, toy, ear, boy, found)
- A piece of paper or a whiteboard to draw the hangman
- Markers or chalk to draw the hangman

Instructions:

1. Choose a word from the list of words and write dashes on the paper or whiteboard to represent each letter in the word (e.g., for "boat," write "_ _ _ _").
2. Have the player guess a letter in the word.
3. If the letter is in the word, write the letter in the appropriate blank space(s) (e.g., if the player guesses "o," write "_ o _ _").
4. If the letter is not in the word, draw a part of the hangman (e.g., the head, body, arms, legs, etc.).
5. Continue playing until the player correctly guesses the word or the hangman is completed.

UNIT 6: VOWEL DIGRAPHS AND DIPHTHONGS

Variations:

- To make the game more challenging, you can use longer words or words with multiple vowel digraphs or diphthongs.
- You can also change the game to guess the vowel digraph or diphthong instead of the whole word.
- Another variation is to play this game in teams, with each team taking turns guessing the letters or digraphs.

Note: Do not move to the next unit until this lesson is mastered.

Unit 7: Silent Letter: Magic E

Objective: Students will be able to identify and understand the role of silent "e" in words.

Materials Needed:

- Whiteboard or chart paper
- Markers or colored chalk
- Word cards with and without silent "e"
- Worksheets

Introduction (5 minutes):

1. Begin the lesson by writing a word with a **silent "e"** on the whiteboard or paper. For example, **hope**.
2. Ask the students if they notice anything unusual about the word.
3. Prompt them to identify the silent "e" and discuss its purpose in the word.
4. Explain that a silent "e" changes the sound of the vowel that comes before it.

Silent e—also called "magic e" or "bossy e"—makes the vowel in a CVC word say its name (long sound) instead of its short sound when an "e" is added to the end.

Here are some examples to help illustrate the concept of **silent e**:

UNIT 7: SILENT LETTER: MAGIC E

Without silent e:

- **hat** (short vowel sound: /a/)
- **kit** (short vowel sound: /i/)
- **hop** (short vowel sound: /o/)
- **tub** (short vowel sound: /u/)

With silent e:

- **hate** (long vowel sound: /ā/)
- **kite** (long vowel sound: /ī/)
- **hope** (long vowel sound: /ō/)
- **tube** (long vowel sound: /ū/)

As you can see, adding a silent e at the end of each word changes the vowel sound from a short sound to a long sound. It's important to note that silent e doesn't always make the preceding vowel long, but it's a helpful rule of thumb for many words in the English language.

Direct Instruction (15 minutes):

1. Explain that silent "e" is used in words to change the sound of a vowel. It tells the reader to make the vowel sound long instead of short.
2. Demonstrate the difference between a long and short vowel sound by writing two words on the board, such as "pin" and "pine". Point out that the "i" in "pin" sounds short, while the "i" in "pine" sounds long because of the silent "e".
3. Give examples of other words that have a silent "e", such as "lake", "time", "made", and "cute". Write each word on the board, and have the students identify the silent "e" and the long vowel sound.
4. Explain that silent "e" is usually found at the end of a word, but there are some exceptions.

Guided Practice:

1. Distribute word cards with and without silent "e" to each student.
2. Have students sort the cards into two piles: one with silent "e" and one without.
3. Have the students read the words with the silent "e" aloud and underline the silent "e".
4. Pair up the students and have them take turns reading words with and without silent "e" to each other.

Independent Practice:

1. Distribute worksheets with words containing silent "e".
2. Have the students read the words and circle the silent "e".
3. Have the students write a short paragraph using some of the words from the worksheet.

Closure (5 minutes):

1. Review the lesson by asking students to explain the role of silent "e" in words.
2. Have students share their favorite word with a silent "e" and why they like it.
3. Encourage students to continue practicing identifying silent "e" in words.

Assessment: Monitor student participation during the guided and independent practice. Check completed worksheets for accuracy in identifying silent "e". Use formative assessments to adjust instruction as needed.

Game-time: Pictionary (Magic E and other Hidden Helpers)
  Materials:

UNIT 7: SILENT LETTER: MAGIC E

- A list of words that contain silent letters (e.g., knife, sign, hour, climb, write, bomb)
- A whiteboard or large sheet of paper
- Markers or chalk to draw the pictures

Instructions:

1. Pick a word with a "magic e" (silent e) at the end from the list (like "cake," "bike," or "note").
2. Draw a picture to show the word without any letters.
3. Show your drawing to the other player(s) and have them guess the word.
4. Once they guess correctly, talk about how the "magic e" changes the vowel sound to make it say its name (long sound).
5. Take turns picking new words and drawing!

Variations:

- **Use Longer Words:** Try choosing words with more syllables that also have silent letters (like "knuckle," "receipt," or "wristwatch") for an extra challenge.
- **Double Up on Silent Letters:** Choose words with multiple silent letters (such as "gnarl" or "plumb"). Draw a picture to represent the word without giving away the silent letters.
- **Play Guess the Silent Letter:** Once the word is guessed, have the other players try to identify which letter(s) are silent and explain why they're silent or what they do in the word.
- **Silent Letter Riddles:** Instead of a picture, give clues about the word, emphasizing its silent letters. For example, "This is something you use to spread butter, and it has a silent 'k.'"
- **Timed Round:** Set a timer to add pressure! The players must guess the word within a certain time, then quickly discuss the role of the silent letter.

- Keep taking turns with these variations to deepen your understanding of silent letters while having fun!

Note: Do not move to the next unit until this lesson is mastered.

Unit 8: Special Consonants

Objective: Students will learn to recognize and produce the sounds of special consonants, including: ch, sh, th, ng, nk, and qu.

Materials:

- Whiteboard or chart paper
- Markers
- Picture cards or flashcards with words containing special consonants
- Worksheets for practice

Introduction (5 minutes):

1. Review the concept of consonants and the sounds they make.
2. Introduce the special consonants ch, sh, th, ng, nk, and qu.
3. Write each special consonant on the board and explain its sound.

Direct Instruction (15 minutes):

1. Using picture cards or flashcards, provide examples of words that contain each special consonant.
2. Have students repeat each word and identify the special consonant.
3. Explain the pronunciation of each special consonant and model how to say each sound.
4. Have students practice saying each sound out loud, focusing on correct pronunciation.

Guided Practice (15 minutes):

1. Distribute worksheets that contain words with special consonants.
2. Instruct students to circle or underline the special consonant in each word and say the sound out loud.
3. Walk around the classroom and provide assistance as needed.
4. **Independent Practice (15 minutes):**
5. Have students create a list of words that contain each special consonant.
6. Encourage them to practice saying each word out loud and focus on correct pronunciation.

Conclusion (5 minutes):

1. Review the sounds of each special consonant.
2. Provide feedback on students' independent practice and offer any additional support needed.
3. End the lesson by having students say each sound out loud one more time.

Game-time: Charades (Special Consonants)
Materials:

- A list of words that contain phonics concepts (e.g., long vowels, short vowels, consonant blends, digraphs, silent letters, etc.)
- A timer
- A piece of paper and a pen

Instructions:

1. Divide the players into two teams and choose a player to go first for Team 1.
2. The player picks a word from the list and keeps it a secret from the other members of their team.

UNIT 8: SPECIAL CONSONANTS

3. The player then acts out the phonics concept for the chosen word without speaking or using props (e.g., for the word "blender," the player could mime blending ingredients together).
4. The other members of Team 1 try to guess the concept of phonics being acted out within one minute.
5. If Team 1 guesses correctly, they get a point. If not, Team 2 gets a chance to guess for the steal.
6. The game continues with each player on each team taking turns acting out phonics concepts and guessing.
7. If players cannot think of a word to act out, they can skip their turn.
8. If a team guesses incorrectly, the word is revealed and placed aside. That word cannot be used again in the game.
9. The game continues until all the words have been used or until a predetermined number of rounds have been played.
10. The team with the most points at the end of the game wins.

Variations:

- To make the game more challenging, you can use longer words or more advanced phonics concepts.
- You can also change the game to guess the word that contains the phonics concept instead of the phonics concept itself.
- Another variation is to allow the actor to use props or make sounds, but only to make sounds that match the phonics concept being acted out (e.g., for the word "bake," the actor could make the sound of an oven or a timer beeping).
- To add a competitive twist, you can set a time limit for each team to guess as many phonics concepts as they can in a certain amount of time (e.g., 5 minutes). The team with the most correct guesses at the end of the time limit wins.

Note: Do not move to the next unit until this lesson is mastered.

Unit 9: R-Controlled Vowels

Objective: Students will be able to recognize and read words with r-controlled vowels and identify the different r-controlled vowel patterns.

Materials:

- Chart paper or whiteboard
- Markers
- Flashcards with words containing r-controlled vowels
- Worksheets with exercises for practice

Introduction (5 minutes):

1. Review the different vowel sounds and patterns students have learned in previous lessons.
2. Explain that today's lesson will be focused on r-controlled vowels.
3. Write the term "r-controlled vowels" on the chart paper or whiteboard.

Direct Instruction (15 minutes):

1. Introduce the 'ar' pattern by writing the word "car" on the chart paper or whiteboard.
2. Sound out the word "car" and have students repeat after you.
3. Explain that the letter "r" controls the vowel sound, making it different from the usual "a" sound.
4. Show examples of other words that follow the 'ar' pattern, such as "star"

and "bar."
5. Have students practice reading the words and identifying the 'ar' pattern.
6. Repeat the same steps for the 'er', 'ir', and 'ur' patterns, using examples like "fern," "girl," and "hurt."

Guided Practice (10 minutes):

1. Use flashcards with words containing r-controlled vowels.
2. Have students take turns reading the words and identifying the r-controlled vowel pattern.
3. Provide feedback and corrections as needed.

Independent Practice (15 minutes):

1. Distribute worksheets with exercises for practice.
2. Instruct students to read the words and fill in the missing r-controlled vowel pattern.
3. Circulate the room to provide assistance and answer questions.

Closure (5 minutes):

1. Review the different r-controlled vowel patterns.
2. Ask students to provide examples of words for each pattern.
3. Encourage students to practice reading and writing words with r-controlled vowels outside of class.

Assessment: Monitor students' progress during guided and independent practice. Use formative assessments such as exit tickets or observation to check for understanding.

Game-time: Hangman (R-Controlled Vowels)
  Materials:

SUPER PHONICS

- A list of words that contain various phonics concepts (e.g., long vowels, short vowels, consonant blends, digraphs, silent letters, etc.)
- A marker or pen and paper to keep score

Instructions:

1. One player selects a word from the list of phonics words and writes it down on a piece of paper, leaving blank spaces for each letter of the word.
2. The other player(s) try to guess the word by suggesting letters one at a time.
3. If the suggested letter is in the word, the player who wrote down the word fills in the blank space with the letter in the correct position.
4. If the suggested letter is not in the word, the player who wrote down the word draws a part of a "hangman" (a stick figure being hanged) on the paper.
5. The game continues with each player taking turns suggesting letters until the word is guessed or the hangman is completed.
6. The player who guesses the word earns a point, while the player who wrote down the word earns a point if the hangman is completed.
7. The game continues with new words and players taking turns until a predetermined score is reached.
8. The player with the most points at the end of the game wins.

Variations:

- To make the game more challenging, you can use longer words or more advanced phonics concepts.
- You can also change the game to match words with the same beginning or ending sound or pattern instead of just the same phonics concept.
- Another variation is to allow players to guess the entire word instead of suggesting letters, but with a penalty for an incorrect guess (e.g., the other player earns two points instead of one).

UNIT 9: R-CONTROLLED VOWELS

Note: Do not move to the next unit until this lesson is mastered.

Unit 10: Syllables and Multi-syllabic Words

Objective: Students will learn the concept of syllables, types of syllables, strategies for dividing multi-syllabic words, and practice identifying and breaking words into syllables.

Materials:

- Whiteboard and markers
- Chart paper and markers
- Word cards with multi-syllabic words
- Worksheet with practice exercises

Introduction (5 minutes):

1. Start by Introducing Syllables: Explain that syllables are the beats or chunks in words. You can clap or tap to show how words break down into smaller parts, making it fun and interactive!
2. Write and Identify: Together, write a few simple words on paper or a whiteboard (like "butterfly," "chocolate," or "wonderful"), and ask your child to help you identify the syllables in each word. Clap or tap for each syllable to make it hands-on!
3. Explore Different Types of Syllables: Explain that syllables come in different types, like:

UNIT 10: SYLLABLES AND MULTI-SYLLABIC WORDS

- **Closed** (ends in a consonant, like "cat")
- **Open** (ends in a vowel, like "me")

Provide Examples Together: For each type, say a word aloud and clap out its syllables. Let children try it on their own with some new words, helping them notice patterns.

Guided Practice (15 minutes):

1. Distribute word cards with multi-syllabic words to each student.
2. Ask the students to identify the syllables in each word and write the syllables on chart paper.
3. Review the syllables with the class and correct any mistakes.

Independent Practice (15 minutes):

1. Distribute a worksheet with practice exercises.
2. Students will identify the syllables in each word and write the syllables in the boxes provided.
3. The teacher will review the worksheet with the class and correct any mistakes.

Closure (5 minutes):

1. Review the concept of syllables, types of syllables, and strategies for dividing multi-syllabic words.
2. Ask students to share any words they struggled to divide into syllables.
3. Ask students to practice dividing multi-syllable words independently and bring any challenging words to the next class.

Assessment: Assess students' understanding of the concept of syllables, types of syllables, and strategies for dividing multi-syllabic words through observation during guided and independent practice, as well as review of the completed worksheet.

Game-time: Silly Sorting
Materials

- A set of multi-syllabic word cards (use Wanderlust Cards or pieces of paper)
- A set of syllable cards (use Wanderlust Cards or pieces of paper)
- Two sorting mats labeled "1 Syllable" and "2+ Syllables"
- A timer (optional)

Instructions:

1. Create a set of multi-syllabic word cards, each containing a word with two or more syllables (e.g., umbrella, chocolate, dinosaur).
2. Create a set of syllable cards, each containing a single syllable (e.g., bat, red, tat, zoo, etc.).
3. Divide the players into teams.
4. The first player from Team 1 draws a multi-syllabic word card and reads the word out loud.
5. The other members of Team 1 work together to divide the word into its syllables and place the appropriate number of syllable cards on the sorting mat labeled "2+ Syllables."
6. If Team 1 correctly divides the word into its syllables and places the syllable cards on the correct mat within 30 seconds, they earn a point.
7. If Team 1 cannot correctly divide the word into its syllables and place the syllable cards on the correct mat within the time limit, the other team (Team 2) gets a chance to steal the point by correctly dividing the word and placing the syllable cards on the correct mat.
8. The game continues with each team taking turns drawing word cards and dividing them into their syllables until all the word cards have been used.
9. The team with the most points at the end of the game wins.

UNIT 10: SYLLABLES AND MULTI-SYLLABIC WORDS

Variations:

- To make the game more challenging, you can use longer or more complex multi-syllabic words.
- You can also change the game to have the players identify the stress or accent in each syllable of the word, adding an extra layer of challenge to the game.
- Another variation is to have the players sort the syllable cards by their phonemes or phonics concepts (e.g., vowel digraphs, consonant blends, etc.) instead of just by the number of syllables.

Note: Do not move to the next unit until this lesson is mastered.

Unit 11: Irregular Words and Sight Words

Objective: Students will be able to recognize and read a list of common irregular words and high-frequency sight words.

Materials:

- List of common irregular words and high-frequency sight words
- Whiteboard and markers
- Practice exercises handouts

Introduction (5 minutes):

1. Start the lesson by asking students if they have ever come across words that don't follow the typical rules of phonics.
2. Explain to them that these are called irregular words and they are commonly used in the English language.

High-frequency sight words (15 minutes):

1. Introduce a list of common irregular words, such as "said," "come," "was," "where," and "have." Write each word on the whiteboard and have students repeat them aloud.
2. Explain that these words cannot be sounded out using phonics rules and must be memorized as sight words.
3. Provide practice exercises where students will read and write the words to help reinforce their spelling and recognition.

UNIT 11: IRREGULAR WORDS AND SIGHT WORDS

Assessment: Observe students during practice exercises and provide feedback and corrections as needed. Administer a written assessment where students will be asked to read and write a list of irregular words and high-frequency sight words.

Extension:

1. Encourage students to read books that contain a high number of irregular words and sight words to help them improve their recognition and fluency.
2. Provide additional practice exercises or games to help reinforce their recognition and spelling of irregular words and sight words.

Game-time: Phonics Boggle (Irregular Words and Sight Words)
Materials

- A set of letter tiles (you can use Scrabble tiles or make your own using cardboard or paper)
- A Boggle grid (you can make your own by drawing a 4x4 grid on paper)
- A timer (optional)

Instructions:

1. Place the letter tiles in a bag or container and shuffle them.
2. Draw 16 tiles at random and place them on the Boggle grid, filling in each square with a single-letter tile.
3. Set a timer for a predetermined amount of time (e.g., 2 minutes).
4. The players try to find as many words as they can using the letters on the grid, connecting adjacent letters vertically, horizontally, or diagonally to form words.
5. When a player finds a word, they write it down on a piece of paper and cross out the letters on the grid that were used to form the word.
6. Players can only use each letter once per word.
7. After the time limit has expired, the players compare their lists and earn

points for each unique word they have found.
8. The game continues with each round using a new set of randomly drawn letter tiles and a new Boggle grid.
9. The player with the most points at the end of the game wins.

Variations:

- To make the game more challenging, you can increase the size of the Boggle grid or use more letter tiles.
- You can also change the game to have players only use certain phonics concepts to form their words (e.g., only words with long vowel sounds or only words with consonant blends).
- Another variation is to have players come up with a sentence or story using as many of the words they found as possible.

Note: Do not move to the next unit until this lesson is mastered.

Unit 12: Reading Practice—Sentences

Objective: Students will practice reading sentences with a mix of phonics concepts.

Materials:

- Sentences with a mix of phonics concepts (prepared in advance)
- Whiteboard and marker (optional)

Introduction (5 minutes):

1. Warm-up: Review Phonics Concepts: Start the lesson by reviewing the phonics concepts covered in previous lessons. You can use flashcards, a whiteboard, or other visual aids to help students review the sounds and spelling patterns.
2. Introduction to Reading Practice: Explain to students that they will practice reading sentences with a mix of phonics concepts. These sentences will include words with different phonics patterns that they have learned in previous lessons.
3. Read Aloud: Read one of the sentences aloud, emphasizing the phonics patterns in the words. Encourage students to listen carefully and identify the sounds they hear.
4. Group Reading: Divide the class into small groups and distribute the sentences. Ask each group to take turns reading the sentences aloud. Encourage students to help each other sound out words and provide feedback on pronunciation.

5. Independent Reading: Distribute copies of the sentences to each student and ask them to practice reading the sentences independently. Encourage students to underline or circle any words they have trouble with and to ask for help if they need it.
6. Partner Reading: Pair students up and ask them to take turns reading the sentences to each other. Encourage them to provide feedback on pronunciation and offer help with any difficult words.
7. Closure: Review the lesson by asking students to share any words they found difficult and how they sounded them out. Encourage them to continue practicing their reading skills at home by reading books and other materials with phonics concepts.

Assessment:

Observe students during group, independent, and partner reading to assess their ability to read sentences with a mix of phonics concepts. Provide feedback and support as needed.

Extensions:

- Encourage students to write their sentences using the phonics concepts they have learned.
- Have students create a game where they take turns reading a sentence, and the other students will have to identify the phonic patterns in the words.

Game-time: Sentence Builder
Materials:

- A set of index cards or small pieces of paper
- A list of simple sentences (with only one or two-syllable words)
- A marker or pen

Instructions:

UNIT 12: READING PRACTICE—SENTENCES

1. Write each word in a simple sentence on a separate index card or piece of paper.
2. Shuffle the cards and place them face down on a table or floor.
3. The first player from Team 1 draws a card and reads the word out loud.
4. The other members of Team 1 take turns drawing cards and placing them to build a sentence.
5. They earn a point if Team 1 correctly builds the sentence within 30 seconds.
6. If Team 1 cannot correctly build the sentence within the time limit, the other team (Team 2) gets a chance to steal the point by correctly building the sentence.
7. The game continues with each team taking turns drawing cards and building sentences until all the sentences on the list have been used or until 8 rounds have been played.
8. The team with the most points at the end of the game wins.

Variations:

- You can use longer or more complex sentences to make the game more challenging.
- You can also change the game to have players use certain phonics concepts (e.g., long vowel sounds, consonant blends) to build their sentences.
- Another variation is to have players develop their own simple sentences using the word cards, which helps reinforce their understanding of sentence structure and basic grammar.

Congratulations!

Dear Supers

Congratulations on completing the phonics workbook! You should be very proud of yourself for all the hard work and effort you put into learning and practicing these important skills.

As you move on to the next stage of your education, remember that these phonics concepts are the foundation for your reading and writing abilities. You now have a strong understanding of letter sounds, syllables, and high-frequency words, which will serve you well as you continue to learn and grow.

But more than that, I want you to remember that you are a Super! You have shown dedication, perseverance, and a willingness to learn that will take you far in life. You can achieve anything you set your mind to, and I can't wait to see all of the amazing things you will accomplish.

So keep reading, keep writing, and keep being the Super that you are. I am so proud of you and know you will continue to do great things.

Love,

Super Aunti

CONGRATULATIONS!

Dear Parents,

You have completed the phonics workbook and have come a long way in developing your child's reading skills. If your child is still struggling with any unit, don't worry. You can repeat the whole book or individual chapters and lessons. Consistency is key, so make sure to work with your child every day to help them retain the information.

If you have tried everything and your child is still struggling, don't hesitate to look into our one-on-one educational therapy. Our experts can help identify specific areas of difficulty and provide personalized support.

In some cases, an Individualized Education Program (IEP) may be necessary to ensure your child receives the appropriate support and accommodations in the classroom. Consider talking to your child's teacher or seeking an evaluation from a qualified professional to determine if an IEP is needed.

Remember, every child learns at their own pace, so be patient and encourage your child to read. With your continued support and dedication, your child will continue to improve their reading skills and develop a lifelong love for learning. Congratulations again on a job well done!

Super Aunti

Dear Educators,

I wanted to take a moment to congratulate you on your commitment to teaching your children using our phonics workbook. Your dedication to your students and their success is truly admirable, and we appreciate your trust in our program.

As you work through the lessons, please remember that every child learns differently, and what works for one may not work for another. It is important not to get frustrated if a child struggles with a particular technique. Instead, alter your approach and try new strategies to help them understand the material.

It is also essential to remember not to try to change the child but to adjust your teaching style to meet their needs. Each child is unique and requires a personalized approach to learning. By recognizing and adapting to their individual learning style, you can help your students achieve success.

Once again, congratulations on your dedication to your students' education. We hope our phonics workbook has been a valuable tool in your teaching journey.

Super Aunti

CONGRATULATIONS!

SUPER PHONICS HERO

This certificate is awarded to:

_____

For successfully completing Super Phonics!

_____   *Super Aunti*
Date   Signature

Bonus: Long Vowel Study Cards

BONUS: LONG VOWEL STUDY CARDS

SUPER PHONICS

sēē

BONUS: LONG VOWEL STUDY CARDS

mēat

SUPER PHONICS

ēats

BONUS: LONG VOWEL STUDY CARDS

hē

hēat

BONUS: LONG VOWEL STUDY CARDS

hēats

SUPER PHONICS

wē

BONUS: LONG VOWEL STUDY CARDS

sēa

sēat

BONUS: LONG VOWEL STUDY CARDS

fēēt

thē

BONUS: LONG VOWEL STUDY CARDS

tēēth

sēa

BONUS: LONG VOWEL STUDY CARDS

sēal

SUPER PHONICS

mēal

BONUS: LONG VOWEL STUDY CARDS

Lēe

SUPER PHONICS

lēaf

BONUS: LONG VOWEL STUDY CARDS

lēast

SUPER PHONICS

fēēd

BONUS: LONG VOWEL STUDY CARDS

fēēl

we'll

BONUS: LONG VOWEL STUDY CARDS

wēēd

SUPER PHONICS

wē'll

BONUS: LONG VOWEL STUDY CARDS

sēals

hēre

BONUS: LONG VOWEL STUDY CARDS

hēre's

rēad

BONUS: LONG VOWEL STUDY CARDS

rēad

SUPER PHONICS

hēar

BONUS: LONG VOWEL STUDY CARDS

rēar

frēē

BONUS: LONG VOWEL STUDY CARDS

thrēē

trēē

BONUS: LONG VOWEL STUDY CARDS

frēēze

thēse

BONUS: LONG VOWEL STUDY CARDS

wēēds

sēēds

BONUS: LONG VOWEL STUDY CARDS

trēat

trēats

BONUS: LONG VOWEL STUDY CARDS

tēēth

SUPER PHONICS

ī

BONUS: LONG VOWEL STUDY CARDS

my

fry

BONUS: LONG VOWEL STUDY CARDS

frīes

SUPER PHONICS

fly

BONUS: LONG VOWEL STUDY CARDS

flīes

SUPER PHONICS

tīe

BONUS: LONG VOWEL STUDY CARDS

īe

dīe

BONUS: LONG VOWEL STUDY CARDS

dry

BONUS: LONG VOWEL STUDY CARDS

sly

SUPER PHONICS

wīld

BONUS: LONG VOWEL STUDY CARDS

mīle

smīle

BONUS: LONG VOWEL STUDY CARDS

smīles

smīled

BONUS: LONG VOWEL STUDY CARDS

wīfe

wīse

BONUS: LONG VOWEL STUDY CARDS

wīde

sīze

BONUS: LONG VOWEL STUDY CARDS

sīde

SUPER PHONICS

rīde

BONUS: LONG VOWEL STUDY CARDS

rīdes

SUPER PHONICS

hīde

BONUS: LONG VOWEL STUDY CARDS

hīdes

try

BONUS: LONG VOWEL STUDY CARDS

trīes

trīed

BONUS: LONG VOWEL STUDY CARDS

seasīde

sēawēēd

BONUS: LONG VOWEL STUDY CARDS

hīgh

mīght

BONUS: LONG VOWEL STUDY CARDS

mīle

flīght

BONUS: LONG VOWEL STUDY CARDS

sīgh

sīght

BONUS: LONG VOWEL STUDY CARDS

līfe

līght

BONUS: LONG VOWEL STUDY CARDS

līghts

līes

BONUS: LONG VOWEL STUDY CARDS

rīse

SUPER PHONICS

rīght

BONUS: LONG VOWEL STUDY CARDS

rīde

trīed

BONUS: LONG VOWEL STUDY CARDS

frīed

SUPER PHONICS

fīre

BONUS: LONG VOWEL STUDY CARDS

fīght

frīght

BONUS: LONG VOWEL STUDY CARDS

āte

hāte

BONUS: LONG VOWEL STUDY CARDS

māde

wāved

BONUS: LONG VOWEL STUDY CARDS

blāze

SUPER PHONICS

safe

BONUS: LONG VOWEL STUDY CARDS

safely

āble

BONUS: LONG VOWEL STUDY CARDS

tāble

tāil

BONUS: LONG VOWEL STUDY CARDS

trāil

SUPER PHONICS

trāin

BONUS: LONG VOWEL STUDY CARDS

tāste

dāydrēam

BONUS: LONG VOWEL STUDY CARDS

SO

SOW

BONUS: LONG VOWEL STUDY CARDS

lōw

blōw

BONUS: LONG VOWEL STUDY CARDS

thrōw

ōld

BONUS: LONG VOWEL STUDY CARDS

sōld

SUPER PHONICS

hōld

BONUS: LONG VOWEL STUDY CARDS

bōld

fōlded

BONUS: LONG VOWEL STUDY CARDS

bōne

rōast

BONUS: LONG VOWEL STUDY CARDS

bōard

food

BONUS: LONG VOWEL STUDY CARDS

fool

SUPER PHONICS

soon

BONUS: LONG VOWEL STUDY CARDS

moon

noon

BONUS: LONG VOWEL STUDY CARDS

room

SUPER PHONICS

loose

BONUS: LONG VOWEL STUDY CARDS

goose

SUPER PHONICS

moose

BONUS: LONG VOWEL STUDY CARDS

tooth

ZOO

BONUS: LONG VOWEL STUDY CARDS

too

to

BONUS: LONG VOWEL STUDY CARDS

do

you

BONUS: LONG VOWEL STUDY CARDS

today

today

BONUS: LONG VOWEL STUDY CARDS

tonight

your

BONUS: LONG VOWEL STUDY CARDS

year

yes

BONUS: LONG VOWEL STUDY CARDS

you'll

you're

BONUS: LONG VOWEL STUDY CARDS

you've

SUPER PHONICS

Rūth

BONUS: LONG VOWEL STUDY CARDS

rūle

rūde

BONUS: LONG VOWEL STUDY CARDS

ūse

fūse

BONUS: LONG VOWEL STUDY CARDS

būgle

SUPER PHONICS

duty

BONUS: LONG VOWEL STUDY CARDS

duties

ruby

BONUS: LONG VOWEL STUDY CARDS

rubies

About the Author

Meet Cree B Good, better known as Super Aunti, a sunny California native whose life is a delightful blend of creativity, adventure, and inspiration! Growing up in Los Angeles, she discovered her passion for music at the tender age of 7, inspired by her father's artistic journey. With a heart full of rhythm, she has carried that love into her role as an educator and author.

After attending college in Alabama, Super Aunti took the exciting leap to New York City, where she passionately supports her son's music career and embraces her role as a stage mom for her two talented young actors. Her life is a whirlwind of performances, rehearsals, and laughter, proving that the stage is truly a family affair!

As the founder of Camp Wanderlust, Super Aunti believes that learning should be as expansive as the world itself. She opened her first learning lab in Los Angeles but quickly realized that the great outdoors held the key to engaging, hands-on education. Now, she and her "Supers" travel far and wide, embarking on cultural adventures that make every trip a treasure trove of knowledge and creativity.

In addition to her work in education and her love for travel, Super Aunti is a passionate author. Her books reflect her belief that learning should be an exciting journey, filled with discovery and joy. Each page is crafted to inspire children to explore, dream, and grow.

With a life that revolves around her children and their shared adventures, Super Aunti brings infectious enthusiasm and a nurturing spirit to everything she does. She's on a mission to make learning unforgettable, proving that every moment is an opportunity for creativity and growth. Join her and her Supers as they embrace the world—one adventure at a time!

You can connect with me on:
- https://www.campwanderlust.org
- https://x.com/campwanderlust
- https://www.facebook.com/campwanderlustnonprofit
- https://www.instagram.com/campwanderlust

www.ingramcontent.com/pod-product-compliance
Lightning Source LLC
Chambersburg PA
CBHW070646160426
43194CB00009B/1605